Other books illustrated by Wendy Anderson Halperin:

HOMEPLACE by Anne Shelby
HUNTING THE WHITE COW by Tres Seymour
THE LAMPFISH OF TWILL by Janet Taylor Lisle
WHEN CHICKENS GROW TEETH
from the French of Guy de Maupassant
retold by Wendy Anderson Halperin

Once upon a company...

A TRUE STORY

BY WENDY ANDERSON HALPERIN

ORCHARD BOOKS   NEW YORK

Orchard Books, 95 Madison Avenue, New York, NY 10016

Manufactured in the United States of America. Printed by Barton Press, Inc.
Bound by Horowitz/Rae. Book design by Wendy Anderson Halperin
The text of this book is set in 13.5 point Galliard. The illustrations are pencil and watercolor
reproduced in full color.   1 2 3 4 5 6 7 8 9 10

Library of Congress Cataloging-in-Publication Data
Halperin, Wendy Anderson. Once upon a company / by Wendy Anderson Halperin.   p.   cm.
Summary: Tells how a seven-year-old boy and his sisters started a wreath-making business,
which, over the course of six years, grew to include other businesses, marketing, wholesaling,
and investing, and netted more than $16,000. ISBN 0-531-30089-7 (trade : alk. paper).—
ISBN 0-531-33089-3 (lib. bdg. : alk. paper) 1. New business enterprises—Juvenile literature.
2. Entrepreneurship—Juvenile literature. [1. Business enterprises. 2. Entrepreneurship.
3. Moneymaking projects.] I. Title. HD62.5.H355 1998 658'.041—dc21 98-13735

DEDICATED TO:

"Everyone who goes for their dreams"—Joel

"Everyone who opens their eyes and thinks big"—Kale

"Everyone who keeps on trying"—Lane

"The exciting thread of education and everyone on
its path"—Wendy

...and to the following friends who helped us to see, to try, to learn,
and to dream:

Duffy • Danny • Jack • Rob • Pat • Dave • Kevin • Devin• Dillon •
Mary Ann • Alice Baltz • R. K. • Elaine • Leonel • Lisa • Monica •
Vincent • Rachel • Jitka • Chuck • Floyd • Joe • Chelsie • Jessica •
Jodi •Andrew • Peggy • Jarrie • Billy • David • Melissa • Mike • Peter
• Teddy • Alice • Mare • Johnny • Heather • Jayme • Liz • Kristi •
Ami • Boppy • Joe • Catherine • Mike • the Beems • Bruce • Rufus •
Mike • Tommy • Emma • Fred • Uncle Irwin • Chrystal • Mr. Martell
• the Averys • Mr. Robinson • Mr. McCreery • Renaissance • the
reporters • Sarah Caguiat • Mina Greenstein • Aunt Julie • Uncle John
• Mr. and Mrs. Gaines • Dominick • the landlord • Richard Jackson •
the whole city of South Haven • all the teachers who buy wreaths every
year • Kalamazoo Public Library • Ellen Carroll Literary Events •
everyone at Orchard Books • the Harborfest Committee • South Haven
Center for the Arts • Emma Miller (top saleskid three years in a row) •
Marion at "A New Leaf" and Rick at Kennicott Bros. Co.

The First Year

Hi, my name is Joel. When I was five, I spent all summer running through the wet, cool sprinkler.

When I was six, I made paper airplanes all day, every day.

When I was seven, my sisters, Kale and Lane, and I went into business.

It all started that November—you know, the time of year when it's really cold out and gloves are sopping wet from the snow, when boots pile up by the door and only hot chocolate can make you feel warm. The time of year when kids like me ask, "Mom, what can we do?"

"Well," Mom said, "you could put on a puppet show for the neighborhood."

"No," I said, "we did that last year."

"You could do a treasure hunt in the tree farm."

"No, our gloves are still wet."

"Well, Christmas is coming up," she said. "You could make wreaths and sell them. There are pine trees everywhere, and I know where we can get a wreath machine."

"Hey," I said, "that's not a bad idea. Mrs. Beem would buy a wreath, I bet, and Mr. Robinson, and maybe—"

"Yeah! We could start a company," Kale cried.

"Let's do it!" shouted Lane.

Boppy, our grandfather, said, "You could start a college fund with the money you earn."

INTRODUCING:

Joel   Kale   Lane   Boppy   Mom

"College?" asked Lane. (She is the youngest.) "What's college?"

"College," Boppy said, "is a place where you can learn about where lizards sleep at night . . .

. . . or what kings and queens eat for lunch, or how Eskimos build houses out of snow. At college, you can learn how to make an eighteen-layer cake or build a rocket to the moon."

Mom said, "It's a place where you're off on your own when you're older, learning all kinds of things."

"College is also expensive," Boppy added. "You often need to save money to pay for it. If you save money, and tell yourself the only thing you're going to spend it on is college, then that money is called a college fund."

And that is how we got our name—The College Fund Wreath Company.

INTRODUCING:

College

Our neighbor, Dominick, runs a Christmas tree farm next door. He lives in Chicago but comes to the farm on weekends to tend his trees. He says he likes to work in the quiet forest and listen to the snow as his boots push through it.

"Dominick," I asked, "after you cut down the trees, could we have the leftover branches to use for making wreaths? We're starting a company."

"Sure," he said, and WE WERE IN BUSINESS!

Nothing smells better than an armful of pine . . . except maybe a whole carful!

Knock, knock, knock. "Hi, we're The College Fund Wreath Company. Would you like to buy a wreath?"

The whole neighborhood gave us orders.

INTRODUCING:

Dominick

We got to work—Boppy, Ami (our grandmother), Mom, Dad, our aunt, our uncle, and all our cousins helped us.

"There must be two feet of snow out there." "Can I stoke the fire?" "I'll clip branches." "How come I'm the only one working?" "Just a minute! After I do this." "We stamped fifty tags!" "Here, have some hot chocolate."

Boppy got us business cards, and we ordered supplies such as wreath rings, red ribbon, and holly berries on 1-800 numbers. It wasn't as scary as we thought.

Newspaper reporters came, and we showed them how to make a wreath. Then we gave it to them.

Orders rolled in.

The first year we made seventy-three wreaths. We gave one to everybody who helped. The others we sold for twenty dollars apiece. After we subtracted the money we'd used to buy supplies, we still had some left over. WE'D MADE A PROFIT! After Christmas, we went to the bank with our money.

Here is a riddle for you:

What has four legs, can rear up on two, eats Christmas wreaths and probably your shoe?

Answer: Our goat.

There are pine trees everywhere and what do you think he eats? Our wreaths! So, if you go into the wreath business, watch out for goats!

INTRODUCING:

Aunt Julie   Ami   Dad   Uncle John   Our Goat   Our Cousins   Reporter

The Second Year

Before we knew it, it was summer. Time for swimming at the beach and playing with our cousins. Time for baseball, Popsicles, and (if we were good) the ice cream truck.

It's also a time when some days are sooooooo *hot* you can hardly move. Your arms feel sticky, everyone is just hanging around, and out comes the question again: "Mom, what can we do?"

"Why don't you guys make a really cool lemonade stand as part of The College Fund Company?"

We knew a good idea when we heard one. We all said, "Hey, yes! We can sell peanut butter and jelly sandwiches too."

Ami is an artist. She makes sculptures. Together, with her help, we made a huge sandwich as our lemonade stand. We got big chunks of Styrofoam, saws, files, liquid nails, concrete (with fiberglass in it), and some paint. We used a sponge to give the concrete the texture of bread. NOW WE WERE ARTISTS!

For the record, be prepared to clean up a giant mess if you make a six-foot-tall sandwich. The Styrofoam gets all over the place. It looked like snow had fallen in the middle of summer. I even got some of it in my teeth!

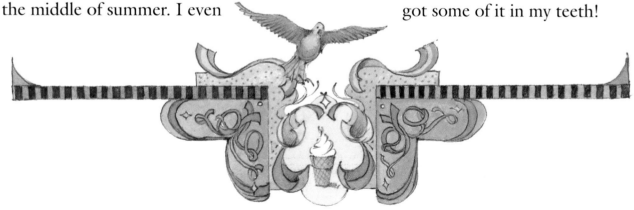

We loaded the stand in a truck Mom had borrowed, and off we went to the Art Fair in town.

"Ice cold lemonade! Peanut butter and jelly sandwiches . . . chunky or smooth!" we called out.

We handed out coupons for a free piece of licorice with P.B. and J. orders. Lane gave one customer forty dollars in change for a five-dollar bill. Luckily the guy told us.

Other kids came by. "Can we help?" they asked. Then they just made themselves at home.

Their mothers chimed in, "Is it okay if Molly and Andrew stay here awhile? I'll be back in about an hour."

Hey, whatever the customer wants—that's our policy.

Work can be fun.

INTRODUCING:

The Customers

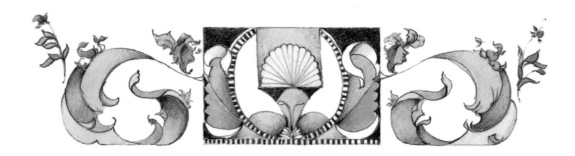

And so The Peanut Butter & Jelly Company was born. Mom kept telling us, "Don't lick your fingers!" How were we supposed to know? We had never made P.B. and J.'s before . . . for other people. But NOW WE WERE CHEFS!

One guy gave us a twenty-dollar tip. He said, "You're going to need it for college."

Some people asked us, "What college do you want to go to?" Or they'd say stuff like, "This will buy one book in college," or "This will pay for one hour or one second of college." We laughed every time, and Mom would say, "Don't worry, you'll get there." We were beginning to understand that education costs money and that we could, and were, helping to pay for it.

At the end of the summer, we cleaned the jelly off our stand, shoes, and shirts, and headed for the bank.

The goldenrod was blooming, which to Lane, Kale, and me always means one thing—school!

Thanksgiving rolled around. Everyone was thinking of turkeys, but we were thinking of wreaths. We got on the phone. "Could we rent your empty store downtown for four weeks for our wreath company?"

"Sure," the landlord said. He gave us a good price (maybe Dad talked to him).

NOW WE WERE MERCHANTS!

We had to go to a "merchants" meeting at 7:00 A.M. (before school). The first meeting in our lives! I even wore a tie. There were coffee cakes, doughnuts, tea, white tablecloths, and questions: "Who are those kids?" "How long have you been in business?" "Will you be open on Sunday?" And, "How late?"

I shoved my tie into my backpack before I got to school.

At the store, we made wreaths, took turns dressing up as Santa Claus, and gave away candy canes. It was a good promotion.

INTRODUCING:

The Landlord   The Merchants

That year we also got our first distributor. Chelsie was seven years old and had just lost her two front teeth. We think that is what helped her sell so many wreaths! She bought them from us for ten dollars apiece and sold them for twenty dollars. We told her that the money had to go toward *her* college fund.

"Okay," she said. "It's a deal."

Our aunt Julie, who lives in Chicago, spoke to Marion, the lady at the flower shop. "My nieces and nephew have a wreath company. Would you like to see what they do?"

"Sure," said Marion, like everyone else.

We got dressed up, and Ami drove us to Chicago. We had a sample wreath to show. NOW WE WERE SALESMEN! Marion liked our wreath so much she ordered sixty to sell in her shop. Unbelievable—suddenly WE WERE WHOLESALERS too! We got all the relatives we could find and the neighbors to help us fill that order. Boppy helped us pack the car. When we went to the bank that winter, we were loaded.

"You guys should get a zero-coupon bond," said Uncle Irwin. We had no idea what that was, but a stockbroker in our town did. He got out his white board and green marker and drew charts of how you can make money grow. You don't plant it or water it. Just save it in a special way—called investing—and in time (years) it can double. NOW WE WERE INVESTORS!

INTRODUCING:

Chelsie	Marion	The Stockbroker	Uncle Irwin	The Neighbors	

The Third Year

We're always thinking of ways to improve our companies. That year we had this idea: We could serve sloppy joes at the P.B. and J. stand. Mom said, "Sounds good." We cooked sixty pounds of ground beef.

"Get another bowl." "Go borrow one from Mrs. Beem." "Where can I put this bowl?" "On top of the birdcage."

Then we called the Health Department for a license. Mike, the guy there, told us, "If you kids serve that beef, you're never going to go to college! What if a fly lands on that sandwich and somebody gets sick? You could be sued and lose your entire college fund, your peanut butter and jelly stand, your *house!*"

We ate sloppy joes all summer; the dogs and the goat had some too. We haven't had a sloppy joe since!

We added Shirley Temples and birthday cake to the P.B. and J. stand instead.

INTRODUCING:

Mike

It was wet gloves, boots piled up at the door, and wreath time again.

One day we were driving along and—*bang*—Mom slammed on the brakes. She'd seen the limb of a pine tree that had fallen and she stopped. We all piled out and stuffed it into the car. "Keeps life, and your wreaths, interesting," she always says. We used to get embarrassed, but we don't anymore.

Kale is really artistic. She loves making stuff. She makes houses for our cat, huge bird beaks you can attach to your face, really cool colored pancakes—and leaves art supplies all over the house. She makes sure the wreaths look beautiful. She puts all kinds of tree branches in them: white pine, juniper, Douglas fir, Scotch Pine, Fraser fir, and different cedars.

When we go out collecting branches for the wreaths, we yell, "Found one," whenever we find a bird's nest. Birds (and our chickens) love to nest in the pine trees.

INTRODUCING:

The Chickens

HARDWARE STORE

The Fourth Year

We're pinecone collectors too.

Pine trees are the easiest trees in the world to climb because the branches are so close together. The pinecones are mostly near the top. We love to go after them. That spring, when we were driving through Georgia, we stopped to get gas and collected seven bags of giant pinecones behind the station.

That summer we added sand art and root beer floats to the P.B. and J. stand. The sand art was a big success . . . but we drank all the root beer floats.

In the fall, we set up the wreath company in Dave's hardware store. When we were not selling wreaths, we played hide-and-seek or horsed around with Dave. "Hey, Lane, want to learn to juggle?" "I bet you can't balance this box on your finger, Joel."

People love to come to that hardware store just to talk. You can run into the whole town there. That is good for The College Fund Wreath Company. Our town is little, but it seems like most everyone buys one of our wreaths.

INTRODUCING:

Dave

The Fifth Year

The next fall, we put an ad in the newspaper. "Sell 10 wreaths, make $100. Earn money for your college fund." I'm telling you, the phone was ringing off the hook. We had to work fast. We set up a desk, an answering machine, a blackboard for orders, an in-and-out mailbox, and all kinds of brochures and stuff. NOW WE WERE SECRETARIES!

"What was Emma's phone number?" "Melissa wants seven twenty-inch wreaths by December 17." "College Fund Wreath Company, Kale speaking." "Will we ever be as big as Wal-Mart?"

We got two more businesses to order our wreaths, and recruited distributors—saleskids, like Chelsie—from all over to make money for their college funds. One was in college already. He was earning money for books. We gave the two top saleskids watches at the end of the season. All the saleskids said, "We're going to start earlier next year."

INTRODUCING:

Our Distributors

The Sixth Year

Now we are so busy that we've had to hire help. WE ARE EMPLOYERS! Our friends work at the P.B. and J. stand for an "all you can eat" arrangement, and we've hired kids and moms to help us make wreaths.

We opened a checking account this year. We keep track of all the dollars, and we pay all of our own expenses (Mom had to help us out in the beginning). We have nails to put receipts on. WE ARE BOOKKEEPERS!

Every year, it seems, there are new challenges. We visited a college to see what everybody's been talking about.

"Hey, Lane, look. All the ice cream you can eat for dessert." "This is the biggest library I've ever seen." "Excuse me, sir, where do lizards sleep at night?"

The other day, Lane said to Mom, "Can I have my own business?"

Mom said, "Well, there must be something. Let's think about that . . . think, think, think."

Since we started The College Fund Wreath Company and The P.B. and J. Company, we have taken in over sixteen thousand dollars. That money is invested and growing. We wrote this book (everyone helped) to let you know that people love seeing kids in business, and kids can help earn money for college.

If you have any ideas . . .

INTRODUCING:

You

GO FOR IT!

The world is your friend.

GLOSSARY

Bookkeeper: Someone who organizes and keeps track of your business expenses and the money that you collect

College: A place where you can continue your education after the twelfth grade or study in more detail the things you are interested in

Distributor: Someone, like Chelsie, who sells the items you make

Employer: Someone who hires workers

Expenses: The amount of money that you spend to buy supplies and make and sell your product (the thing you want to sell). For example, if you have a lemonade stand, and it costs $3 to make your lemonade and $1 to make and put up signs telling folks about your stand, then you add: $3 cost of making lemonade

$$\begin{array}{r} +\$1 \text{ cost of making signs} \\ \hline \$4 \text{ your expenses} \end{array}$$

Health Department: A government organization that checks the food you buy or sell to make sure it's safe to eat, and the stand or restaurant where the food is prepared to see if it is clean

Investor: Someone who saves money in a special way and tries to make it grow by putting it in stocks, bonds, or in the bank

Liquid Nails: A kind of glue. It comes in a cardboard tube with a nozzle that you put in a special holder. You cut the nozzle and squirt out the glue.

Merchant: A person who owns or manages a shop

Profit: The amount of money left over from selling something after you've subtracted the cost of making and selling it. For example, you open a lemonade stand. It costs a total of $4 to make the lemonade and put up signs. You spend all day selling it and take in $10. You subtract: $10 the money you took in

$$\begin{array}{r} - \ \$ \ 4 \text{ cost of making the lemonade and the signs} \\ \hline \$ \ 6 \text{ your profit} \end{array}$$

Promotion: Ideas that you use to help draw attention to your product (the thing you want to sell) and help you to sell it better. For example, if you are selling lemonade and want even more customers to come to your stand, you might offer a free face painting with every lemonade.

Retail: Retail items are items that are directly bought by, or directly sold to, the customer in small quantities for the normal everyday price

Salesman, Salesperson, or Saleskid: A person who goes out into the world and sells your item

Secretary: Someone who is responsible for the telephone, paperwork, orders, bills, and other important tasks in your business

Wholesale: Wholesale items are items that are bought or sold in larger quantities for less than the normal everyday price. A wholesaler is someone who sells items in this way, usually to a store, which, in turn, sells the items at a higher price—or retail—directly to the customer.

Zero-Coupon Bond: A special way to save your money and have it grow by the time you go to college